THE EVERYTHING KIDS' SPIES

PUZZLE AND ACTIVITY BOOK

Follow the clues, go undercover,
and explore the intriguing world of secret agents

Scot Ritchie

Adamsmedia
Avon, Massachusetts

EDITORIAL
Director of Innovation: Paula Munier
Editorial Director: Laura M. Daly
Associate Copy Chief: Sheila Zwiebel
Acquisitions Editor: Kerry Smith
Production Editor: Casey Ebert

PRODUCTION
Director of Manufacturing: Susan Beale
Production Project Manager: Michelle Roy Kelly
Prepress: Erick DaCosta, Matt LeBlanc
Interior Layout: Heather Barrett,
Brewster Brownville, Colleen Cunningham,
Jennifer Oliveira

An Everything® Series Book.
Everything® and everything.com® are registered trademarks of F+W Publications, Inc.

Published by Adams Media, an F+W Publications Company
57 Littlefield Street, Avon, MA 02322. U.S.A.
www.adamsmedia.com

ISBN 10: 1-59869-409-X
ISBN 13: 978-1-59869-409-3

Printed in the United States of America.

J I H G F E D C B A

Cover illustrations by Dana Regan.
Chapter Opener illlustrations by Kurt Dobler.
Puzzles by Scot Ritchie.

This book is available at quantity discounts for bulk purchases.
For information, please call 1-800-289-0963.

See the entire Everything® series at *www.everything.com*.

Contents

DEDICATION

This book is dedicated to Lindsay—the best friend a guy could have and the best photographer, too.

Introduction

Who's that suspicious-looking caveman hiding in the bushes? Could he be spying on you? It's quite possible. From what we can tell, spies have been around as long as we've been walking on two feet. We do know they were around in ancient Egypt. Cleopatra wanted to visit Caesar one day, but she knew spies were looking for her. So she rolled herself up in a carpet and had herself carried into the city of Alexandria! People will do crazy things to get what they want, and sometimes that means being sneaky. As long as somebody wants to know his neighbor's business there will be undercover agents.

What spies do is find information that is supposed to be a secret. Then they pass that on to their boss, or the person that hired them. The boss can be anyone from the government to a business to a spouse trying to find out if his or her partner is playing around on the side. Once the bosses have the information, they can do many things with it—like protect their country in times of war, defend themselves from criminals, or take that no-good scoundrel to court with those interesting new photographs.

There are all kinds of ways to spy. Some old techniques look primitive to us now, but they did a great job at the time. Julius Caesar used a special kind of writing that only he and his friends could read. In fact, he used it so much they even named it the Caesar Cipher. In the Middle Ages, spies would shoot secret letters—literally—to their allies, using a bow and arrow. Don't try and catch that message! In our attempts to outsmart our enemies we have even used animals to spy for us—from dolphins to bats to hamsters. Have you ever thanked a pigeon for all the battles they helped us win?

Every culture has its own type of spy—in Japan they are known as ninjas—but they all do pretty much the same thing. Throughout history, kings, queens, prime ministers, and presidents have all hired secret agents. They all want to see what the competition is doing. Sometimes they've had to kill people—these spies were known as assassins. It's a dangerous business!

If you ever thought you would like to spy, you better be good at observing and memorizing. Often documents are destroyed right after reading them so there is no evidence left. Spies in the movies (like James Bond or Austin Powers) are always in danger of getting killed, so the most important thing for them to remember is—don't get caught! Of course gruesome and dramatic ways of putting secret agents to death usually only happen in the fictional world. In real life, assassins are a lot more secretive. History is full of secret agents who have died under suspicious and mysterious conditions.

As technology improves, so do undercover methods. Hot air balloons and horses that were used to get across enemy lines have now given way to computers and cell phones.

People have always been fascinated by the world of spies and espionage. Imagine having your very own secret language! Or working with spy robots defending the border of countries at war.

With *The Everything® Kids Spies Puzzle and Activity Book*, you can break into the world of secret agents and see what goes on behind the laser beams and night-vision lights. So get your sunglasses and let's go spy!

The EVERYTHING KIDS' SPIES Puzzle and Activity Book

Chapter 1

SPYcial Effects–
Spies in the
Movies and on TV

Bond, James Bond

James Bond never existed in real life, but thanks to movies, books, cartoons, and video games, he is the most successful spy ever.

How many times can you see 007 written on James Bond's car? Will you score 007 or 000?

What happened to the spy who slept under his car?

Get Smarter!

Only some of these spies work together. You can tell by the numbers on their chest. Can you find the 4 spies who add up to 99?

One of the first comedy spy shows on TV was called *Get Smart!* The stars were Maxwell Smart (Agent 86) and his partner (who never had a real name), Agent 99.

Groovyyy . . .

This spy is a lot of fun to watch.
Can you figure out who it is?

Lights, Camera, Spy!

Spy movies go back a long way—all the way to 1914! To find out the name of the first spy movie ever made, fill in the spaces with 2 dots.

The EVERYTHING KIDS' SPIES Puzzle and Activity Book

In the Shadows

There's someone lurking in the shadows.

There are 6 spies but only 1 shadow; which one matches?

You can make your own shadow games. All you need is a strong light!

I Spy with My Little Eye

Can you fly your spy jet to the eye in the middle of the maze?

I Spy was a popular TV show about two top agents working for the CIA.

What's missing here?
Can you see what all these letters have in common?

fl, dr, sp, cr, wh

The EVERYTHING KIDS' SPIES Puzzle and Activity Book

Live + Let Lie

Some of the henchmen below are real characters from the James Bond movie *Live and Let Die*. Others are liars. Can you tell which is which?

Whisper

Shouter

Rosie Carver

Boo Hoo Wilson

Ruby Cutter

Tee Hee Johnson

Earl Lundi

Baron Samedi

What happened in 1961 and won't happen again until 6009?

Mall Mission

This spy is phoning headquarters from the mall, so she's talking in code. Can you figure out what she's saying?

One of TV's first spy shows was called *Mission Impossible*. The heroes fought evil dictators and crime lords around the world. The most famous line from the show was "This tape will self-destruct in five seconds."

The EVERYTHING KIDS' SPIES Puzzle and Activity Book

Spy on the Run

Sometimes you have to run in circles to track down a clue. Can you see why this spy crossed the playground?

Start at the star and collect every second letter. But which way do you go?

Top Secret Tools

In Japan some spies are called ninjas. Can you unscramble the letters below to see some of the tools they use?

Take one letter from each column starting on the left. Each letter can only be used once, so cross them off as you go.

v	r	i	f	s
k	o	a	e	s
t	n	d	e	e
c	i	d	p	o

V.I.P. SPY

There were many women spies on TV, but only a few were the star of the show. Valerie Irons was the spy in *V.I.P.*, a spoof spy show loosely based on previous shows like Remington Steele and the James Bond movies. She always got the bad guy in the end with lots of laughs along the way.

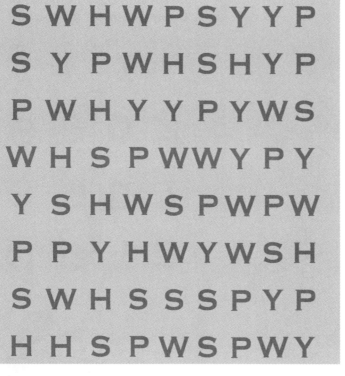

S W H W P S Y Y P
S Y P W H S H Y P
P W H Y Y P Y W S
W H S P W W Y P Y
Y S H W S P W P W
P P Y H W Y W S H
S W H S S S P Y P
H H S P W S P W Y

Hidden in this pile of letters you will find the words SPY and WHY two times each. They can be spelled forward, backward, or even diagonally, so look out!

The EVERYTHING KIDS' SPIES Puzzle and Activity Book

Saintly Spy

The Saint was a very popular movie and TV series that started in the 1930s. The character was played by many different actors, but the most famous was Roger Moore. This detective has just received a new gun. Before he opens it, can you tell which gun he got?

E+E is spy talk for escape and evasion.

Spy at Sea

Ace Ventura: Pet Detective was the name of a movie about an eccentric detective who only worked with lost pets. He was searching for a pet dolphin named Snowflake. Just like a snowflake, these words are not identical—but they look very similar. Each is a one-syllable word that rhymes with the other.

What do you call . . .

. . . a vessel sitting on the water?

. . . a heroic ripple at sea?

. . . the dream of an animal with gills?

. . . the predator of the sea, with a tan?

. . . a very warm sailing boat?

Chapter 2

SPYwear–How to Walk, Talk, and Dress Like a Spy

Dress Up Disguise

A spy needs a good disguise. Can you see which outfits go together?

Careful there are some extra!

During the Cold War, the Russians made a gun disguised as lipstick. Careful putting that on!

Why did the spy cross the road?

Tick, Tick, Tick . . .

Nasty Dr. Nasty
has hidden a bomb.
Can you follow the clues
and diffuse it in time?

1. The real bomb is in a row with a bird in it.
2. The real bomb does not have a heart in the same row.
3. The real bomb has a bird below it and beside it.

Egyptian Espionage

Codes have been used ever since ancient Egypt, and probably long before. In this code each letter is given a number (a = 1, b = 2, and so on). Can you figure out what message this Egyptian spy is about to send?

Egypt, like many other countries around the world, is still spying today. Recently they launched a satellite that can transmit photos of objects only 13 feet wide.

Spies in the House . . .

One of a spy's best tricks is disguise. Go through the maze picking up letters on the way. When you are finished, you will see what disguise these spies are wearing.

The **EVERYTHING KIDS'** SPIES **Puzzle and Activity Book**

Night Vision

One of these people is a spy whose job is to return the stolen painting in the gallery back to its rightful owner. But before doing anything, the spy has to know as much as possible about the gallery, the guards, and the visitors. There's a lot to remember. Let's see how you do. Look at the picture for one minute and remember as much as you can. Now cover the scene with a piece of paper and see how many questions you can answer.

1. How many people are wearing sunglasses?
2. What does the sign say?
3. Does the guard have the gun on his right or left side?
4. What is the other painting of?
5. How many people are talking on their phones?
6. How many people have backpacks?
7. Is the moon full?

See You Laterrrrr . . .

This spy didn't plan ahead. Can you connect the dots to see what's waiting for him below?

In Spanish this animal is called *el lagarto*. Do you know what that means?

The EVERYTHING KIDS' SPIES Puzzle and Activity Book

Dumpster Diving

You don't have to wear a tuxedo to be a spy. Garbage is one of the best sources of information about a person. In fact "Dumpster diving" is believed to be the #1 method of spying. And it's all legal! The best way to stop snoops from learning about you from your garbage is to use a shredder. Can you put these pieces back together and read this top-secret message?

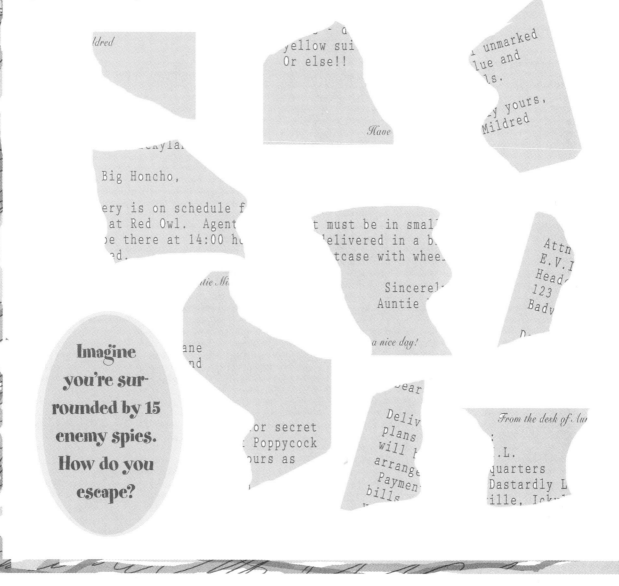

Gadget Magic!

A good spy never leaves home without at least 3 gadgets. Can you see how many our spy has?

Scientists who developed the first atomic bomb had a special nickname for it. Do you know what it was?

The word *gadget* is believed to come from the French word *gachette*.

The EVERYTHING KIDS' SPIES Puzzle and Activity Book

Sp-eye Glasses

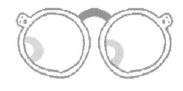

Want to know how to read this secret message? Write down only the letters in the glasses with a dark left lens. This will tell you who to meet at the bridge at noon.*

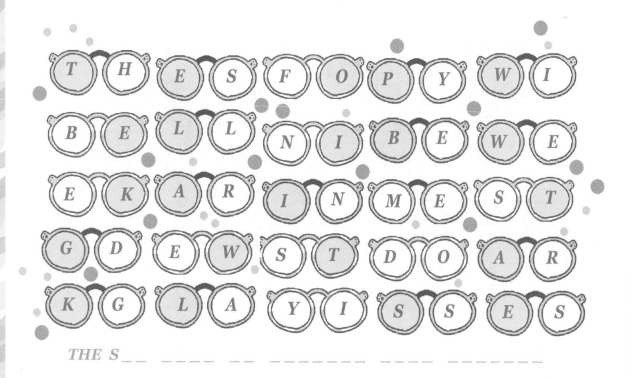

THE S__ ____ __ _____ ____ _____

There was an explosion at the eyeglass factory.
Every single person was trapped, but two people escaped.
How is that possible?

*We've started you off with the first two

What Are You Looking At?

What you look like is just as important as what you're looking at in the spy biz. This bumbling secret agent is so busy watching us he hasn't noticed his cover is upside down. **Can you spot the 10 differences in the newspaper photos?**

What kind of ring does a spy give when he's going to get married?

?

Spy Buster

When a spy stays overnight somewhere new, he wants to be sure he is really alone. Now there's a gadget where he can look through the lens and scan the room for hidden cameras. If there are any, they will reflect back a flashing red dot. Can you see what is revealed when these dots are joined together?

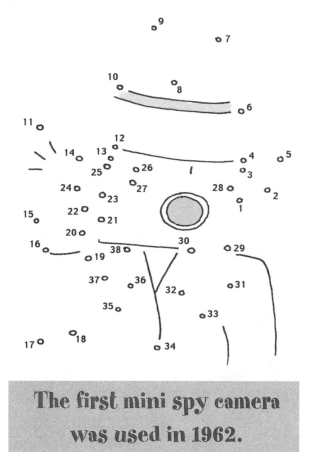

The first mini spy camera was used in 1962.

Spy Sweep

This secret agent is about to go in and "sweep" the office. But she's not doing what we think of as sweeping. Do you know what this spy term means?

Dusting the room looking for fingerprints

Inspecting for bugging devices and cameras

Having a short nap

Installing energy-efficient lightbulbs

Deadly Do-Right

Spies get to see a lot of strange things. One of the weirdest is seeing a dead body in the equestrian posture. This causes the body to sit upright with arms outstretched—just like it was sitting in a saddle!

To find out what causes this, fill in all the letters that are not M, O, I, R, G, T, and S and read the remaining letters.

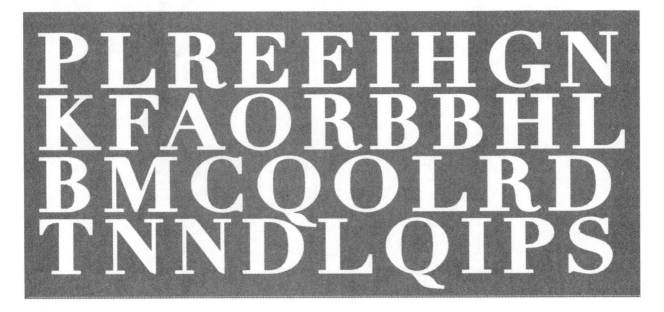

PLREEIHGN
KFAORBBHL
BMCQOLRD
TNNDLQIPS

Chapter 3

Chirp, Squeak,
and Grrrr!–
Animals That Spy

Hear Kitty Kitty!

Which kitty has only the following: two stripes on his tail and a mark on his right eye, right back paw, left front paw, and both ears?

The CIA had plans to put bugging devices in cats to find out the secrets of the Kremlin. But the first cat they released was run over by a taxi. That cat definitely didn't have nine lives!

Can you read the secret message?

SPY CAT

Licensed to Smell

Start

Can you find your way through the happy rats and angry rats all the way to the happy rat at the end? Just alternate between happy and mad. You can go sideways or up and down but not diagonally. And if you run into a sleeping rat, you're going the wrong way. Okay, hold your nose and let's get going.

End

Gerbil Alert!

Tiny, four-legged agents were placed in cages at security areas at the Tel Aviv airport to sniff out terrorists. Gerbils can detect an increase in adrenalin—that could mean a terrorist. The police abandoned the operation when they realized gerbils couldn't tell the difference between a terrorist and a nervous passenger.

Sneaky Storks

Can you find your way through this flock of storks?
Look out for those long legs.

I think there's a spy among us.

In Burundi, a country in East Africa, a stork was fitted with a tracking device to spy on the travel patterns of other storks.

Finally!

Now we know the answer to the age-old question:
Which came first, the chicken or the egg?
Here's a clue—who was around millions of years ago?

The EVERYTHING KIDS' SPIES Puzzle and Activity Book

Doggy Don't

If you want to leave a clue for a doggie spy don't use color, because they're color blind. But dogs have an amazing sense of smell, 50–100 times more powerful than our own. Can you help Fido find the right flower?
It must have the following characteristics:

6 petals
2 leaves
No face
No stripes
A heart

Doggy Doo

A homing device was made to look like doggie doo. It works great because nobody wants to go near it!

Who's Watching Who?

The spy behind the lamp is supposed to be getting a message from the pigeons, but they are moving all over the place. Can you put them in order and make a sentence?

Secret Mission

This secret agent is going on a mission. Can you tell what he's bringing with him?

(a)

 + et

p +

vest

(b)

(c)

Pigeon Crime!

Connect the dots and see some hardened criminals in a place you wouldn't expect.

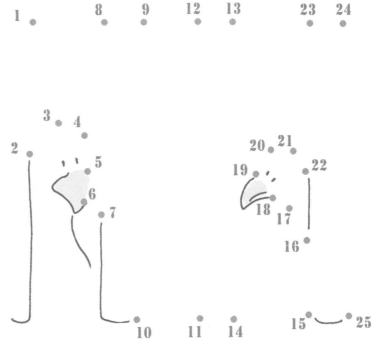

Cold Clues

A secret agent was looking for a criminal. This took him far away from the city. One day he headed out of his camp and walked 3 miles straight south, then he turned and hiked 3 miles due east. Finally he turned again and walked 3 miles straight north, where he was surprised to see a big bear breaking into his cabin. What color was the bear?

Cold War, Warm Bomb

What time is it when 10 spies are chasing you?

How many chickens can you find on the bomb? During the Cold War, when everybody was spying on everybody, things got a bit crazy. Plans were made by the British army to put chickens inside nuclear land mines to keep the bombs warm during the cold winters. It was dubbed the "Chicken Powered Nuclear Bomb." Plans were cancelled when they realized the chance of nuclear fallout was too great.

Act like a chicken

Here's a fun game you can play with the gang or just a few friends. Tell them it's very important to stay in character and think like chickens. Here's the story: You're chickens in your henhouse having a normal day when all of a sudden a bomb is coming your way. **How would you act?**

Pigeon Mission
Grounded!

Can you help this carrier pigeon find her way home?

One reason carrier pigeons were used during the war was because of their speed. How fast can a carrier pigeon fly?

1. 30 mph
2. 50 mph
3. 90 mph

In the 1970s the CIA tested how much weight a carrier pigeon could carry. They were loaded with such heavy surveillance cameras that they had to land and walk home!

Spy Sharks!

There are three sharks swimming around. Can you spot them?

Scientists plan on using sharks to carry cameras to search hostile waters ahead of U.S. troops. Sharks have a sense we don't even have, called "electrosense." They can "see" electrical fields made by other living things.

What's in the middle of a jellyfish?

Follow the Lion Line

Sea lions, because of their great endurance and speed, are used as underwater detectives in the U.S. Navy. They patrol offshore waters, keeping an eye open for enemy intruders. Can you figure out which line the lion on the left has to follow to catch the intruder? You can travel along any one, but the one with the lowest score is the correct answer.

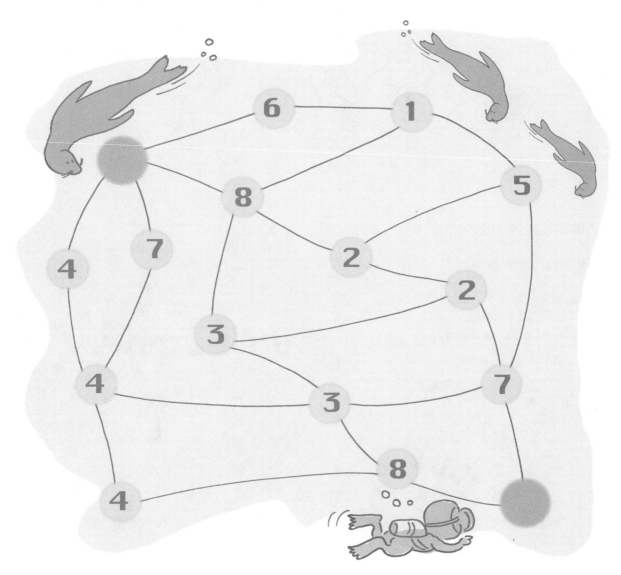

Bird Brains

More than 30 military pigeons won the Dicken Medal during the Second World War. What is it for?

A: Mission accomplished

B: Time spent in the air

C: Bravery

D: Ability to decode messages

One of the most well-known pigeons was honored by the Lord Mayor of London with the Dicken Medal of Gallantry for missions he flew in Italy. What was his name?

Ruhr-Express

GI Joe

Snow White

Scotch-Lass

10601

Spy at Sea

This spy is getting some help from a dolphin after an accident at sea. Can you recognize what this was before it got blown apart?

TALK the TALK

Spies have a lot of phrases only they understand—that way they can talk in public and still keep their secrets. Can you figure out which meaning goes with which phrase?

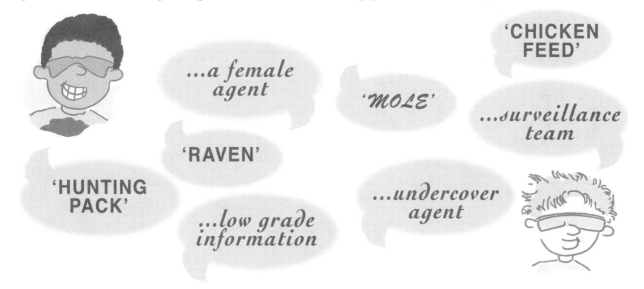

'CHICKEN FEED'

...a female agent

'MOLE'

...surveillance team

'RAVEN'

'HUNTING PACK'

...undercover agent

...low grade information

Cool Spy Facts

Top Secret!

Spies use all sorts of special methods to do their work:

A **dead drop** is the delivery of information from one person to another, without the two people actually meeting. The two people agree on the delivery location ahead of time, and then they use secret signals to communicate. This way, no one can tell what they're doing!

Concealment devices are used to hide one object inside of another less suspicious object. Books are perfect for this. You can cut a hole in the pages and place an item inside. When the book is closed, no one can tell there's something hidden there!

False flag operations are events staged by one group in order to make it appear as if another group (usually the enemy) is responsible. The term comes from the military practice of flying the flag of another country on your ship so no one knows your true identity during wartime.

The EVERYTHING KIDS' SPIES Puzzle and Activity Book

Chapter 4
Ye Olde Spye-Famous
People Who Used Spies
or Were Spies
Through History

Dot, Dash, D'Oh!

Can you figure out this code,
what does the message say?

A	1	J	10	S	19
B	2	K	11	T	20
C	3	L	12	U	21
D	4	M	13	V	22
E	5	N	14	W	23
F	6	O	15	X	24
G	7	P	16	Y	25
H	8	Q	17	Z	26
I	9	R	18		

16,12,5,1,19,5
19,5,14,4
13,15,14,5,25!

Before computers some businesses used Morse code to
send messages only they could understand. Telegrams
were so expensive they were also sent in code.

**You can make your
own alphabet. Here
are some symbols to
get you started . . .**

a	b	c	d	e	f	g	h
i	j	k	l	m	n	o	p
q	r	s	t	u	v	w	x
y	z						

Double Cross

See if you can spot the double-crossing double agent. They all look the same at first, but only two are exactly alike.

In the Second World War the British Military Intelligence used the double cross system—also known as XX System. They would release Nazi prisoners back to Germany with false information. One of the most famous agents to work this way was code named Tricycle.

Name That Code

This undercover agent is at a secret location where documents have been left for him. There's a special name that spies have for this type of delivery. Can you figure it out?

1. The 1st letter in the code name is between C and E
2. The 2nd letter in the code name is the 5th letter of the alphabet
3. The 3rd letter in the code name is in data and special
4. The 4th letter in the code name is the same as the first
5. The 5th letter in the code name is in dot and dash

6. The 6th letter in the code name is the 18th letter in the alphabet
7. 7th letter in the code name looks just like a number
8. The 8th letter in the code name is in plane but not trace

___ ___ ___ ___ ___ ___ ___ ___
 1   2   3   4   5   6   7   8

Detective to the Rescue!

Time to put on your spy hat. There are 4 documents below, each divided into 4 quarters. Can you detect which quarter in each document doesn't belong?

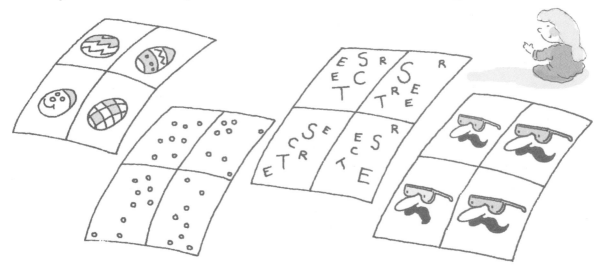

Spy Camp

This campground is a mess! Can you put the two halves back together? Just draw a line from one half of a tent to its other half.

James Armistead was an African American slave who volunteered to spy for the army. He had the perfect excuse—he would sell the British food. His spy work was instrumental in helping the American patriots achieve victory.

Don't Be Left Hanging!

Often called America's first spy, Nathan Hale is best remembered for his famous line "I only regret that I have but one life to lose for my country." He is said to have spoken these words moments before being hanged.

See if you can avoid the hangman and find out who he was spying on. Finish the sentences below using the words in the list on the right. Each of these words has one capital letter in it—that's the one you write down to find out who Nathan Hale was spying on.

If you're working for both sides you're a _____ agent.

One of Nathan Hale's first jobs was as a _____ .

Another name for an operation is a _____ .

A spy is also known as a _____ agent.

The U.S. security service is called the _____ .

If you dress up like somebody else it's called a _____ .

You saved a life, you're a _____ !

Nathan Hale was a _____ in the army.

If the enemy captures you, you're a _____ .

A _____ distracts from the real thing.

The place they hang people is called the _____ .

Somebody you don't trust is called a _____ .

To light a bomb you need a _____ .

secreT

capTain

douBle

Hero

decOy

susPect

fuSe

diSguise

mIssion

c.I.a.

pRisoner

gallOws

teacheR

The EVERYTHING KIDS' SPIES Puzzle and Activity Book

Medieval Messenger

All this Medieval secret agent has done is switched 3 letters and made this message almost impossible to read. Can you figure it out? Or if you want some help, look at the bottom of the page. Geed luck!

TWO FACES

If you're a spy, it helps to have more than one face. Can you see the two faces here—happy and worried? Check the answer to see how you can make your own happy/sad face.

YEU MILL BO WOT BY RIS SANDELPH EN HIR HESRO. YEU WURT BO SOADY TE SIDO TE THO WIDDLO EF TEMN AT WIDNIGHT RATUSDAY! *THIR IR MRITTON IN CEDO

E for O
M for W
S for R

Caesar Cipher

Cipher is another word for code. This cipher was named after Julius Caesar because he sent secret messages where one letter was replaced with another. Can you decipher what he's saying?

Why did Caesar cross the road?

Here's a fun activity. You can dress up like a spy even if you don't have sunglasses and a trench coat. Just think of all the spies in history. If you want to be Caesar, all you need is a bed sheet and a belt. The rest is history!

The EVERYTHING KIDS' SPIES Puzzle and Activity Book

Speedy Spartans

Forward + drawkcaB

Can you read this message? Read every second letter, then when you're finished start reading backward to the start to get the whole message. Write down the letters as you go and you'll soon see the message meant for the Spartan king!

What letter comes next in this sequence? M, A, M, J, J, A, S, O?

Spartan leaders would sometimes burn secret messages into long strips of leather. The messenger would then wear it as a belt so he could get through enemy lines without anybody noticing anything unusual.

Spy Queens

Can you spot how many magnifying glasses and eyeglasses are hidden on Queen Elizabeth's dress?

Even queens used spies!

Queen Elizabeth I used spies to stop a plan to overthrow her and replace her with Mary Queen of Scots.

The EVERYTHING KIDS' SPIES Puzzle and Activity Book

The Scarf Knows

During World War II some spies were given fashionable scarves that could protect them from the wind and rain. But more importantly they were printed with maps showing nearby towns, roads, and escape routes. These 2 scarves go together. One is a map, the other is a decoder. Can you figure out where this spy should go to escape?

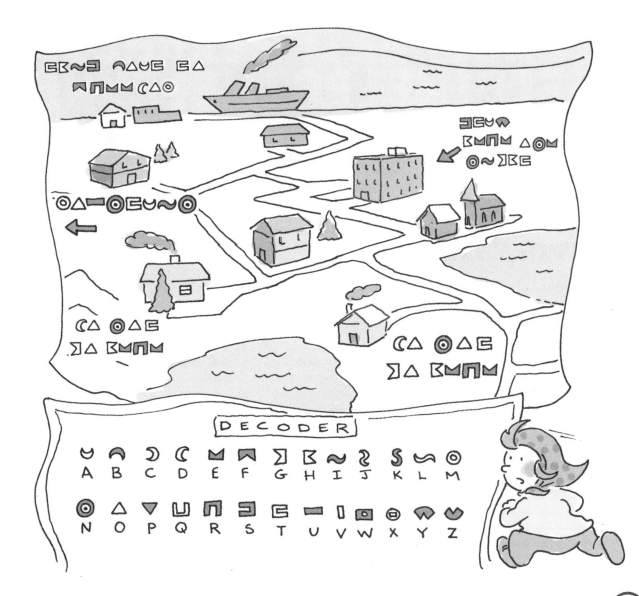

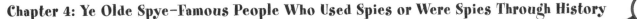

What, What?

Many spies suffered a great deal of torture if they were captured by the enemy. Can you make out what this poor secret agent is saying? Color in the H-E-L-Ps to reveal their words.

HELPHELPHELPSTHELP
OPHELPHELPHELPHELP
HELPIHELPGIHELPVHE
LPEHELPHELPHELPUP!

Currency Affair

Can you break this substitution code and figure out the riddle?

23-8-1-20   8-1-19   1 8-5-1-4,   1 20-1-9-12,   9-19
2-18-15-23-14 2-21-20   8-1-19   14-15 12-5-7-19?

The EVERYTHING KIDS' SPIES Puzzle and Activity Book

Chapter 5

What Was Your Name Again, Miss?–Famous Female Spies

Muddled Mail

Belle Boyd was a Confederate spy during the Civil War. She rode through enemy lines to deliver vital information.

Can you deliver this urgent message to the general? The only route that works is the one with all the correct letters to spell Belle Boyd. Giddyup!

Crossword Cross Border

Harriet Tubman was the first American woman to lead a military operation. The raid freed 750 slaves. She was a slave herself and went on to work as a spy helping slaves escape to Canada.

Read the clues and see how many you can get.

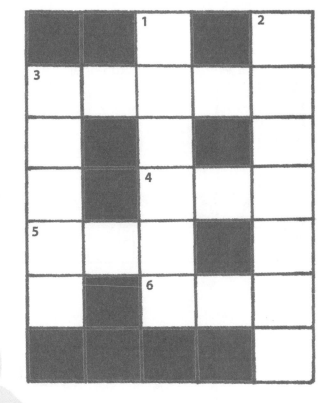

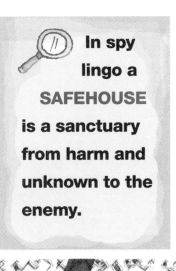

In spy lingo a **SAFEHOUSE** is a sanctuary from harm and unknown to the enemy.

Across

3. Somebody owns you
4. Not one but . . .
5. The night before
6. Walk don't . . .

Down

1. The person in charge
2. A brave woman is a . . .
3. Watches secretly

Coded Crossword

Most spies had code names so the enemy never knew who they were. "Madeleine" was the code name for Noor Inayat Khan, a descendent of Indian royalty who wrote children's stories. She was a radio operator who spied on the Germans and helped defeat the Nazis.

Across

1 If you break it, you can use it

7 Not stop but . . .

9 If you're from Moscow, you are . . .

18 I can't tell you; it's a . . .

Down

1 What spies search for

5 Not lost but . . .

7 It's what you play

C.I.Eh?

Can you help this spy avoid a trap? She has to connect the correct country with it's own spy agency but somebody has mixed them all up.

France
India
Russia
Canada
Vietnam
USA

CBI
KGB
CIA
CONG AN BO
CSIS
DGSE

The Lady in Gray was a cartoon spy from *Mad* magazine's popular comic strip called "Spy vs Spy"—she was always setting traps for the main characters, Black and White.

The EVERYTHING KIDS' SPIES Puzzle and Activity Book

Shark No More

Julia Child, a famous gourmet chef, once worked with the OSS (a U.S. spy agency). She invented a shark repellent used to keep sharks away from floating bombs meant to sink German ships.

Which platter has the exact same critters as the one in the center?

What's that smell?

See who can make the smelliest repellent from things in your kitchen. What would sharks hate? But don't get in trouble—better ask permission first.

Silly Spy Sayings

Is she talking code or just being silly? See if you can figure out the first letter of these silly sayings.

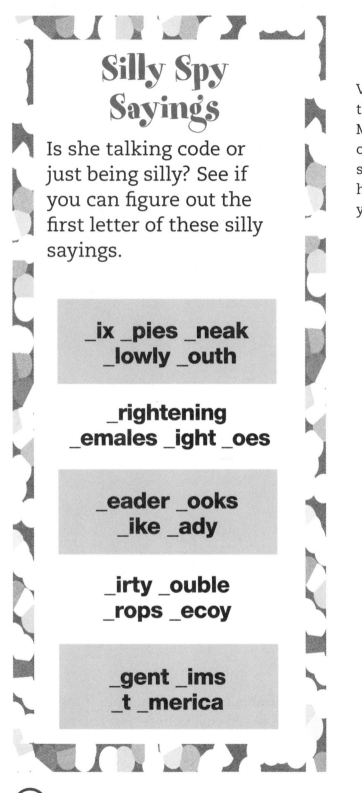

_ix _pies _neak _lowly _outh

_rightening _emales _ight _oes

_eader _ooks _ike _ady

_irty _ouble _rops _ecoy

_gent _ims _t _merica

The Great Escape

Virginia Hall was an American spy fighting the Nazis. She escaped over the Pyrenees Mountains. This would be difficult for anyone but was especially hard on Virginia—she had a wooden leg after losing it in a hunting accident years before! Can you find your way through this mountain maze?

START

FINISH

The EVERYTHING KIDS' SPIES Puzzle and Activity Book

Spy Dance

Mata Hari was believed to be a double agent during World War I working for France and Germany. She was a dancer who mingled with the rich and famous. Although the evidence to condemn her was suspicious, she was executed by firing squad on October 15, 1917.

Mata Hari is sending a secret message to a spy in the audience. Can you find these 12 objects hidden on the stage? Envelope, clock, bomb, radio, cup, pen, bird, snake, ruler, bell, hat, shoe.

Untie the Spy

These spies were all ready to go out on the town but that rotten Dr. Dastardly has tied them all up. . . . If you can spy the two that are exactly alike, they can escape.*

*The direction they are facing isn't counted as a difference.

The Sploosh Game

Everybody gets in a circle and follows what the person before them says by adding one more spy, like this:

"One spy, two legs. Sploosh!"

"Two spies, four legs. Sploosh, Sploosh!"

"Three spies, six legs. Sploosh, Sploosh, Sploosh!"

You've Been Warned!

Kate Warne was America's first female detective. She was the first woman to be hired by the Pinkerton Agency, and she had a key role in stopping an assassination attempt on President Lincoln. She went on to form an all-female unit of Pinkerton's called the Female Detective Bureau.

Pinkertons

How many words can you find in this word? You can only use a letter once per word. We found 25—but there's even more for the persistent sleuth.

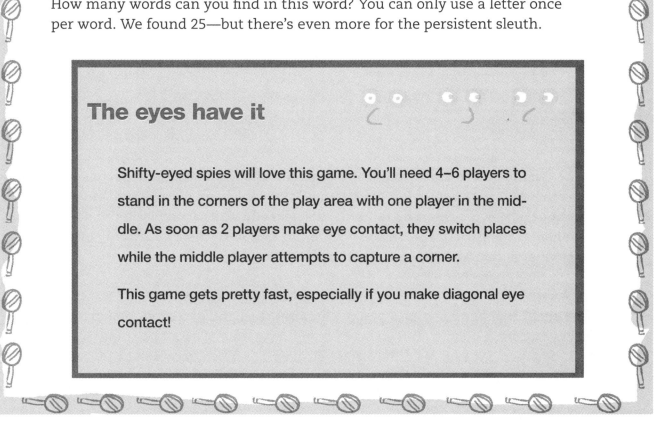

The eyes have it

Shifty-eyed spies will love this game. You'll need 4–6 players to stand in the corners of the play area with one player in the middle. As soon as 2 players make eye contact, they switch places while the middle player attempts to capture a corner.

This game gets pretty fast, especially if you make diagonal eye contact!

And the Award Goes To . . .

An actor, a clown, and a spy have a lot in common—each one wears costumes to hide their identity. And these three are very picky—they will only wear certain clothes. Can you figure out what they would wear? We've started you off with a couple of examples . . .

Actor

Bow Tie, Dressing Gown

Spy

Bikini, Robe

Clown

Shawl, Kilt

APRON   LOINCLOTH   KIMONO   SKI SUIT

HAT   RAIN COAT

BOARD SHORTS   CAP   HOODIE   OVEN MITT

CAPE   BEANIE

SPACE SUIT   DAISY DUKES   TOGA   COAT

BLOUSE   SWEATPANTS

Pauline Cushman was an actress who decided to change careers and become a spy during the American Civil War. When battle plans were discovered hidden in her shoe, she was sentenced to hang. It is said she was saved just three days before her hanging, but because she went on to tour with the PT Barnum circus, a lot of what is said about her now is thought to be exaggerated.

That's Funny!

An FBI agent was interviewing a bank teller after the bank had been robbed three times by the same bandit. "Did you notice anything special about the man?" asked the agent. "Yes," replied the teller. "He was better dressed each time."

Starstruck!

Josephine Baker was a singer and dancer in the 1920s. She was so famous in Europe that people checking passports were starstruck. They never thought she might be a spy. She was able to smuggle information about the French Resistance across borders written in invisible ink on her sheet music!

It looks like the person who started to write this song had to leave in a hurry. Can you help finish it off?

♫ **A TRIP TO PARIS**

THE PLANE LEAVES TO-----

IT'S A LONG DARK F------

TOMORROW IT WILL BE L------

AND PARIS WILL BE A GREAT S------!

*Hint: all the words rhyme

What kind of glasses do spies wear?

Cool Spy Facts

William Somerset was a famous spy from Paris. Born in 1874, then orphaned as a child, he lived in England for most of his childhood. Somerset initially studied medicine, but turned to writing in his twenties. He didn't have a typewriter and spent hours writing his novels and plays by hand.

In 1917, during the Russian Revolution, the British Secret Service recruited Somerset as a secret agent. His job was to go to Russia and distribute counterfeit German pacifist propaganda. Though his sole mission as a spy failed, Somerset turned the experience into a series of novels that supported him financially for the rest of his life!

Not a crocodile but an . . .
ALL _ _ _ _ _ _

It makes you sneeze
ALL _ _ _ _

A narrow street
ALL _ _

To let do something
ALL _ _

To attract
ALL _ _ _

All Star!

Moe Berg was a baseball-playing spy who took movies of the harbor from the top of a Tokyo hospital in his kimono. He wasn't the best catcher, but he was a great spy.

The words on the left start with "ALL" and on the right with "STAR"

To frighten
STAR _ _ _

To be very hungry
STAR _ _

Looking directly
STAR _ _ _

A small bird
STAR _ _ _ _

It has five arms
STAR _ _ _ _

Can you hit a home run and figure them all out?

The EVERYTHING KIDS' SPIES **Puzzle and Activity Book**

$pyPay

These top-secret envelopes have been ripped in half. When they're put back together with their proper half, they add up to $100. Count the total in each half envelope and write it next to it.

Why did the spy cross the road?

Great Gizmos!

Can you deduce which gizmo comes next?

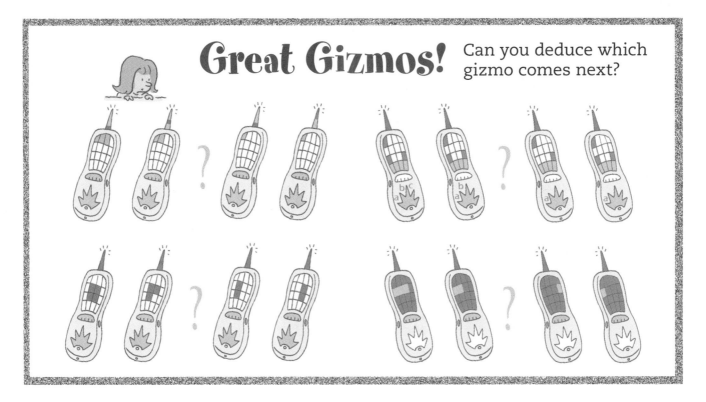

Secret Sight

Write a letter in the middle space to finish the 11 vertical words. Then you can see two words spelled horizontally that tell you what helps a spy see when the sun goes down.

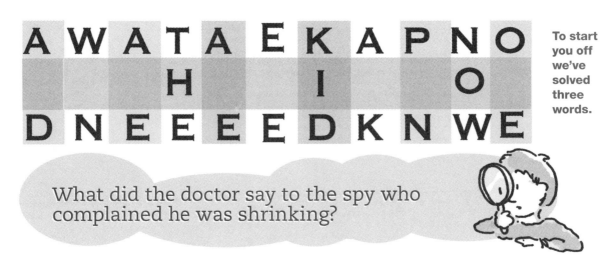

A W A T A E K A P N O

   H   I   O

D N E E E E D K N W E

To start you off we've solved three words.

What did the doctor say to the spy who complained he was shrinking?

The EVERYTHING KIDS' SPIES Puzzle and Activity Book

License to Spy

Can you read these license plates? They all have something to do with spying—except for one—can you figure out which one it is?

ICE PIE
4 U

SOUP R
SEEKRAT

S.P.O.
NAJ

GR8
W8ER

CUVR
UNDR

DISK EYES
X PRT

Slaphappy Spy

You have to have fast reactions if you're a spy. You never know what's around the next corner. Here's a game you can play with your friends. All players get down on their knees with their hands flat on the floor. Taking turns, each spy slaps the ground. If you miss, you're eliminated. The faster you go the better! If you want to make it more difficult, add a silly phrase everyone has to say with each slap—like *"Gadget Gizmo!"*

Spy School

Here's a spy lesson using a whole alphabet—can you match the object with the letter? Each letter from A to Z is represented.

Sir William Stephenson was a Canadian spy who passed important information to Winston Churchill and Franklin Delano Roosevelt. He set up a school in Canada called Camp X, the first training school for secret wartime operations in North America. One of the graduates was Ian Fleming, who went on to write the James Bond books.

Name Game

Spies come in all shapes and sizes. Here are some spy names from A to Z with the first letter missing. Use the whole alphabet—but you can only use each letter once:

Cross out the letters as you go

A B C D E F G H I J K L M N
O P Q R S T U V W X Y Z

_uke

_laine

_eter

_iranda

_olanda

_ictor

_rian

_hris

_erry

_ulie

_ony

_avier

__ac

_endy

_ave

_am

_rank

_uth

_uentin

_ancy

_rville

_ma

_an

_arry

_llan

_elly

Sidney Reilly was known as the Ace of Spies. He was the real-life spy believed to be used as the model for Ian Fleming's James Bond series.

Secret List

heLmet
radiO
Camera
motorbiKe

fRame
clOthes pin
draPes
newspapEr

Dish
Ink
pantS
Gum
soUp
slIppers
Screen
rulEr

Bathing suit
cOokies
fOlder
jackeT
sunglasSes

bLanket
cAndle
fiSh
pEncil
eRaser

"Executive action" is what spies call assassination.

This spy is doing some shopping. But he's not getting what you might think. Can you tell what he's really going to buy?

The EVERYTHING KIDS' SPIES Puzzle and Activity Book

The Spy Twins

There are 12 differences
between the 2 spies.
Can you spot them?

*The word spy comes from
the French word espionage.*

Four spies are listed below.
Only 2 of them really existed.
Which ones are real?*

A	T	A	M
I	R	A	H
H	T	A	N
A	H	N	A
A	L	E	L
B	S	E	M
T	D	N	O
O	Y	K	O
E	S	S	R

How observant are you? There are 6 spies on this case, so there should be 6 of every thing. Can you see what 3 items don't show up 6 times?

Six Spies

Risky Business

Spying can be a very dangerous business. Hugh Redmond, a CIA agent, spent almost 20 years in a Chinese prison. Before he was captured he worked in Shanghai, in disguise, as an ice cream machine salesman.

What do you serve that you cannot eat?

How many ice cream cones can you see hidden in this picture?

Spy Facts

The Cambridge Five

The Cambridge Five was a group of five English students who were accused of giving confidential government secrets to the Soviets during World War II. Some people have also suggested that they passed false Soviet information to the Germans.

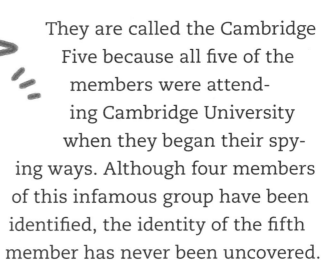

They are called the Cambridge Five because all five of the members were attending Cambridge University when they began their spying ways. Although four members of this infamous group have been identified, the identity of the fifth member has never been uncovered.

The EVERYTHING KIDS' SPIES Puzzle and Activity Book

Chapter 7

Look Out for That Catfish!—Weird and Crazy Spy Stories

Ancient Agents

Eavesdropping was frowned on among ancient Anglo-Saxons. People who hung around the "eavesdrip" of another person's home were punished with a fine. The eavesdrip was the area around the house (about 2 feet) which received the rain falling from the eaves.

Can you figure out how this ancient Anglo-Saxon spy got from start to finish on this roof?

START

FINISH

The EVERYTHING KIDS' SPIES Puzzle and Activity Book

Bird's-Eye View

Can you help the 5 chicks at the bottom of the page find their real mothers out of all the birds in this mixed-up flock? Careful, some of the markings look very similar.

Now we can spy on migrating birds with the aid of **NEXRAD (Next Generation Radar)**. This system is meant to track weather but has proved very useful in seeing where and when birds migrate.

In Britain, "birdwatcher" is slang for "spy."

Double Trouble

These agents are looking both ways for trouble. Your challenge is to make it from start to finish without getting tied up

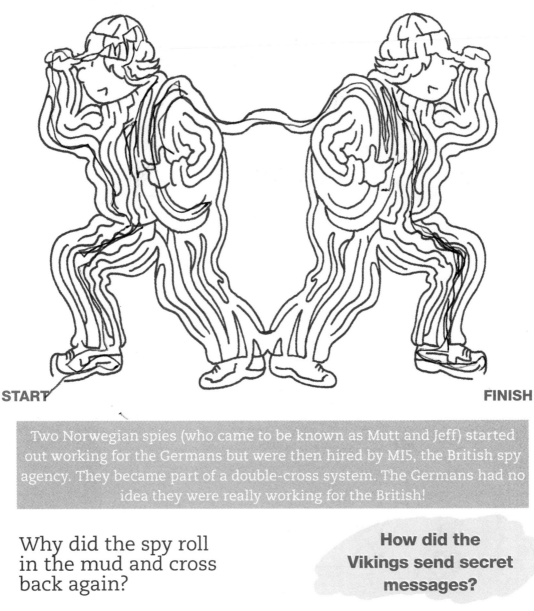

START

FINISH

Two Norwegian spies (who came to be known as Mutt and Jeff) started out working for the Germans but were then hired by MI5, the British spy agency. They became part of a double-cross system. The Germans had no idea they were really working for the British!

Why did the spy roll in the mud and cross back again?

How did the Vikings send secret messages?

The EVERYTHING KIDS' SPIES Puzzle and Activity Book

Country Code

Spies travel all over the world, so they have to know their geography. Can you unscramble these country names?

CANFER _____

LTAYI _____

HAaINC _____

NAAJP _____

PIANS _____

RAIN _____

EREGEC _____

KSTAINAP _____

DAINI _____

RIBAZL _____

GLENDAN _____

AADACN _____

Now place the letters in the boxes in their correct order to see which country has the coldest spies.

☐ ☐ ☐ ☐ ☐ ☐ ☐

In Plain View

There are 5 words written here in plain view. You just have to figure out where to start.

A Head of His Time

Can you see what this tattoo is? Just join the dots, starting at #1.

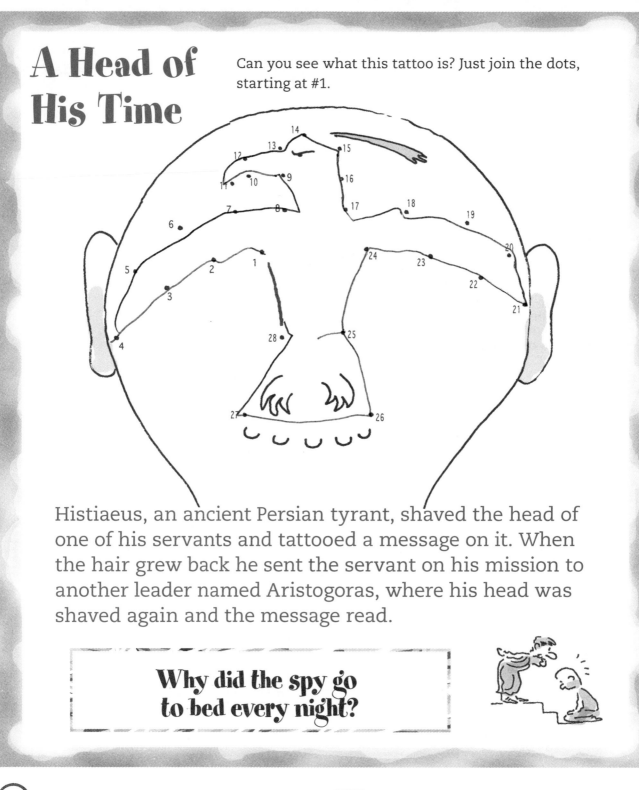

Histiaeus, an ancient Persian tyrant, shaved the head of one of his servants and tattooed a message on it. When the hair grew back he sent the servant on his mission to another leader named Aristogoras, where his head was shaved again and the message read.

Why did the spy go to bed every night?

The EVERYTHING KIDS' SPIES Puzzle and Activity Book

Don't Look Now

See if you can figure out what evil man in history had a double* so his enemies could never be sure exactly where he was. Here's what you have to do: Fill in these squares:

- All the way down the left sides of 1, 4, 5, and 6
- All the way down the second panel from the left of 2 and 3
- All along the bottom of 4 and 5
- All the way down the far right side of 1
- All along the top of 3, 5, and 6

*A "double" is a person who looks very much like the person you are trying to protect.

"Ears only" means the material is too secret to commit to writing.

"Eyes only" is a spy term having to do with documents that may be read but never discussed.

Micro What?

Can you find the 3 words hidden in these letters? Take one letter from each row, going left to right until you reach the end of the letters. They all mean "small."

During the Cold War a special microdot camera was invented. The camera was tiny, but the photos were even smaller. So small they could fit inside the period at the end of this sentence.

**PITILE
METUTE
LINTTE**

Heads Up!

Benita von Falkenhayn was a German baroness who was found guilty of espionage and treason and sentenced to death. She was one of the last people in Germany to be beheaded with an axe.

These heads have got all mixed up. Can you see who goes where?

It's a Bird, It's a Bee, It's a Plane!!!

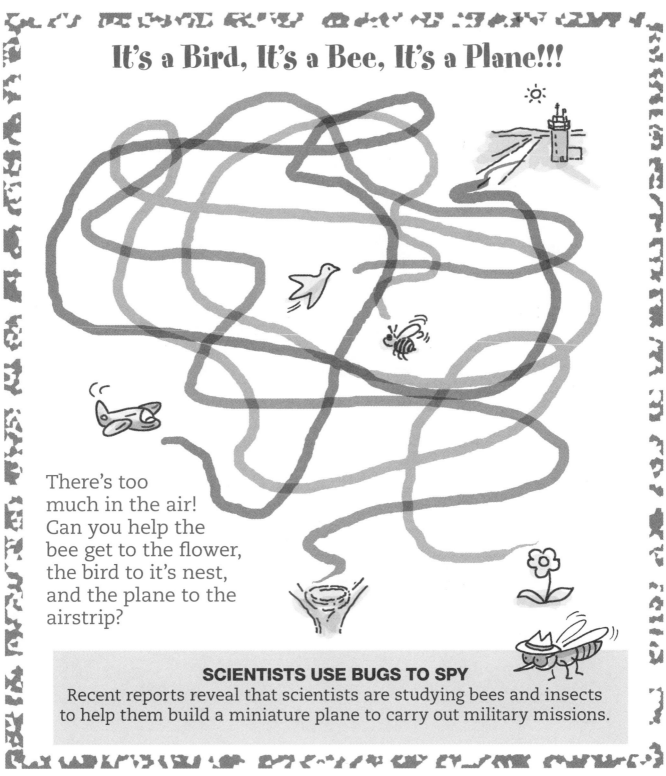

There's too much in the air! Can you help the bee get to the flower, the bird to it's nest, and the plane to the airstrip?

SCIENTISTS USE BUGS TO SPY
Recent reports reveal that scientists are studying bees and insects to help them build a miniature plane to carry out military missions.

Skeleton Secrets

The Trow Ghyll skeleton was found in a cave in Yorkshire, England, in 1947. Some people believe it to be the remains of a German spy.

Flushleght

stids

taethbrosh

witch

hindkorchoof

shoving taba

cimposs

faintoun pin

bix ef motchus

Here are some of the things that were in the cave with the skeleton. But somebody has mixed up all the vowels—can you figure out what they found?

What does a skeleton say before it eats dinner?

Inside Job

Robots are being used more than ever in the world of spies because they can be repaired if they get in an accident.

It looks like this robot has lost its motor. Can you spot which one fits?

Close Call

This spy is using a new gadget—binoculars with a camera attached. It looks like she hasn't figured out the proper setting because her pictures are too close.

Can you make out what she is spying on?

Cool Spy Facts

Who Created James Bond?

Ian Fleming was the creator of one of the most famous spies, James Bond. But did you know that Mr. Fleming was also a spy himself?

Personally recruited by the Director of British Navy Intelligence in 1939, Fleming's codename was "17F." It was even rumored that he trained at Camp X, a secret school at which Allied forces trained during World War II. The codenames for his assignments include "Operation Ruthless," "Operation Overlord," and "Operation Goldeneye." Sound familiar?

Chapter 8

Gear + Gadgets—
From Underwater to
Up in a Helicopter

Gadget Girl

The word *gadget* is believed to come from the French word gachette, meaning a catch piece of a mechanism.

Mirror Code

Can you make any sense of this top secret message? Here's a tip: a mirror will make it much easier to read. Write down the capital letters in the secret phrase to find out the name of the man who invented the telegraph—the first form of electric impulses sent across a wire.

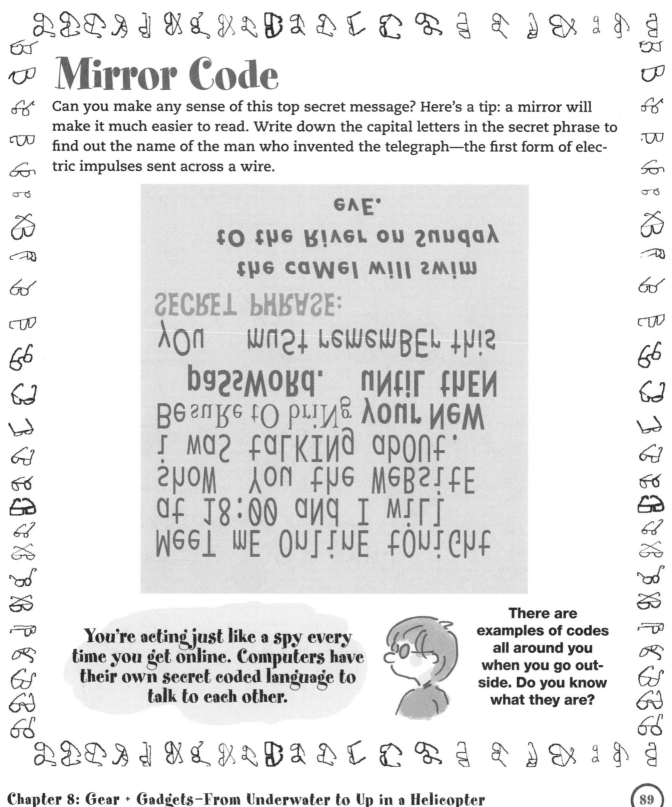

You're acting just like a spy every time you get online. Computers have their own secret coded language to talk to each other.

There are examples of codes all around you when you go outside. Do you know what they are?

When Bats Attack!

Bats were going to be used to carry bombs, but the army decided against it when they escaped, blew up the general's car, and set fire to the barracks.

Here are some words that were used to describe brave spies at war. But the words have been blown apart. Can you put the pieces back together?

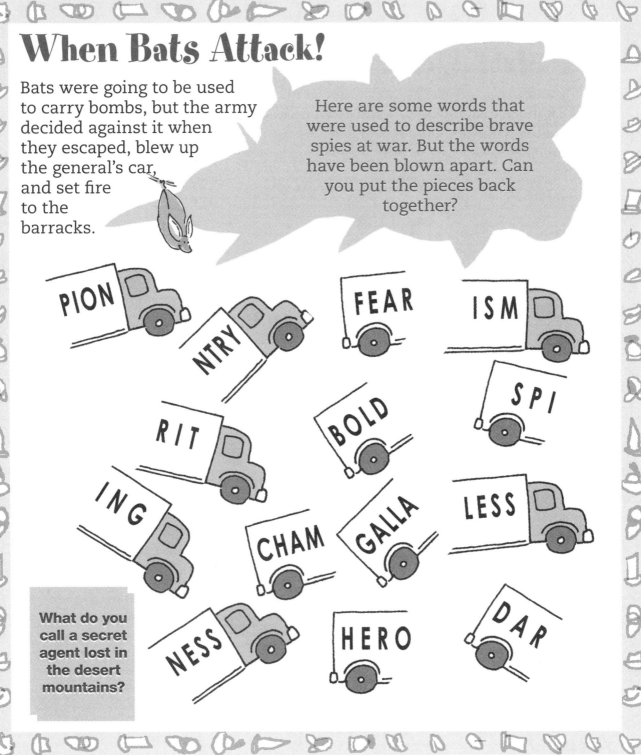

PION

NTRY

FEAR

ISM

RIT

SPI

BOLD

ING

CHAM

GALLA

LESS

NESS

HERO

DAR

What do you call a secret agent lost in the desert mountains?

The EVERYTHING KIDS' SPIES Puzzle and Activity Book

Trace That Call

Can you trace the way through to your contact inside the maze?

Your cell phone can be used as a tracking device. It's against the law for anyone to do this, but be careful what you say!

Activity:

Invisible Ink

1. Pour lemon juice in a bowl. Dip a toothpick in it and with the lemon juice write your message.

2. You can see the lemon juice on the paper only when it's wet. When it dries it's invisible!

3. When you want to read your message hold it over a light bulb and the ink will turn brown. The hotter the light bulb the better, so be careful.

Killer Spy Robots

South Korea has designed a robot to guard its border with North Korea. The robot uses voice recognition to decide what to do after asking "Who goes there?" It can sound an alarm, fire rubber bullets, or use its machine gun.

How good are you at detecting differences? This robot is looking at himself in the mirror . . . but something is not quite right.
Can you see the 14 differences here?

How does a little spy go to work?

Cat Vision

Night vision glasses let you see what's going on when there is no light. Just like a cat. Or in this case, a cat burglar.

Get your crayons and see if you can find all the things listed below. Color them in as you find them. This cat burglar has been very busy!

1 each: Airplane, dog, dress, fork, candleholder, CD player, TV, watering can, footstool, mirror, picture frame

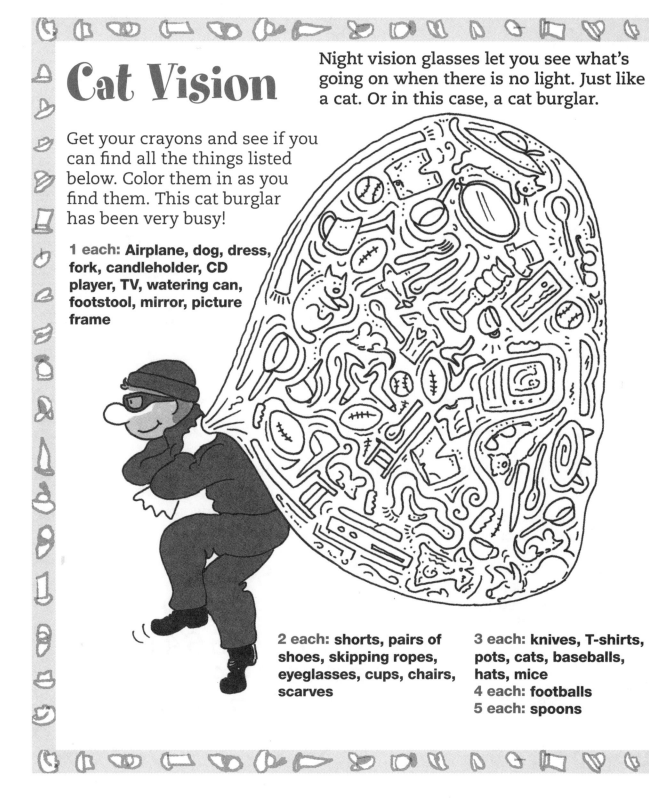

2 each: shorts, pairs of shoes, skipping ropes, eyeglasses, cups, chairs, scarves

3 each: knives, T-shirts, pots, cats, baseballs, hats, mice
4 each: footballs
5 each: spoons

Robot Spies

In 2000 the CIA built a robot that looks exactly like a certain type of animal. Its exact purpose is still top secret but experts believe the robot is used to collect water samples near suspected nuclear or chemical sites.

Can you figure out what it is?
Just collect the capital letter in each word and write it on the line below.

6Secret   7cHemical

              4liFelike

5devIce   1nuClear

              2reAlistic

3roboT

___ ___ ___ ___ ___ ___ ___
 1   2   3   4   5   6   7

Raise the Flag

Find out another term spies use to describe someone who puts up a false front to hide his true identity. Fill in the numbers and read the letters that remain to see the answer.

If you are a spy, one thing you definitely don't want to hear is that you have been BLACK FLAGGED—it means you would be interrogated and shot!

347F559A77L
394S98569E3
6F9923564L4
447689A2288
234G7768992

Hack Attack!

Answering machines are a great way to say hi, but they're not the most secure way to leave a message. In fact they're very easy to "hack."* Can you make out what this message says? Somebody has got in and mixed it all up!

ME YOU HOME
TO GET CALL
AND GO CAN
WE WHEN
MALL THE.

*To illegally break into a computer or other device.

Footfall

A gadget used by lots of spies is the footfall detector. It senses vibrations as we walk.

There are a whole bunch of footprints here, but only one of them matches the shoe. Can you detect which one it is?

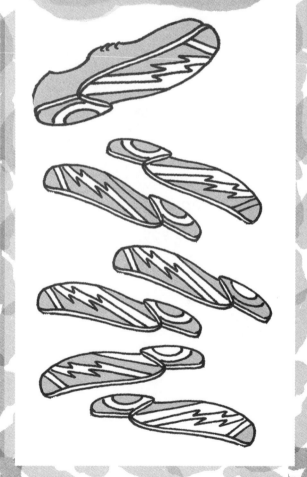

Great Gadgets!

This is something every spy wants! Fill in the blank spaces using words from the list. Then write the one capital letter from each word on the line at the end of the sentence. Now put them in the correct order to find out what every spy wants but only a few can afford.

A _____ distracts from the real thing.

The U.S. Security Service is called the _____ .

The _____ machine encoded messages during WWII.

A U-turn made during a car chase is a _____ .

If you're working for both sides, you're a _____ agent.

The _____ are the Canadian police agency.

Some Japanese spies are called _____ .

If you're a spy, it helps if you're _____ .

List:

dEcoy	ciA	eNigma
fliP	ninjaS	
sneakY	doubLe	rcmP

Seeing Double

Spies don't just wear sunglasses to hide their identity, they also use them to see who's behind them. Now there are spy sunglasses with mirrors inserted in the rims—so they can look forward and backward at the same time!

There are 18 spies in this scene—all trying to hide their identity. Can you find the two fake spies? They're wearing identical sunglasses.

If two's company and three is a crowd . . . what are four and five?

Chapter 9

Spy-Fi—What the Future of Spying Could Look Like

Seagull or Spyplane?

Researchers in Florida have created flying drones that mimic the wing action of seagulls. They are designed to morph shape in mid-flight and can shoot darts with microphones into targeted areas.

Can you find the bird/plane hidden in these geometric shapes? Get out your crayons and color it in.

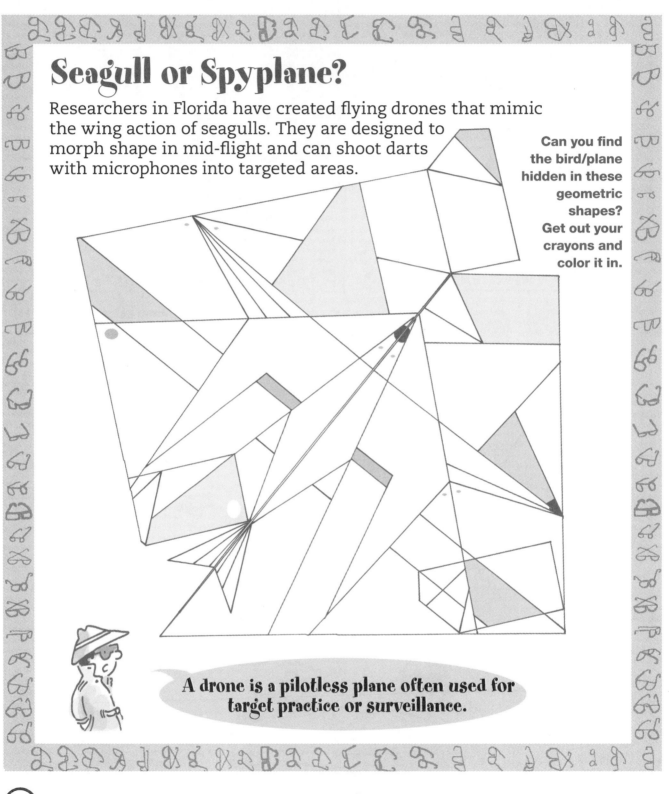

A drone is a pilotless plane often used for target practice or surveillance.

The EVERYTHING KIDS' SPIES Puzzle and Activity Book

Secret Cipher

Here's a great cipher you can do yourself. It was created during the Civil War by a Union prisoner to send messages, but it can still be used today. Instead of writing the letter, just write the shape around the letter. Can you see what this future spy has written on his bedroom door?

A "code" is a system of symbols, numbers, or signals that conveys information.

A "cipher" is a written code where letters are substituted according to a system.

Future Spy

In the future when spies are working in space they will need new uniforms. Here's a group of secret agents flying on a mission. But one of them doesn't fit. Can you pick her out?

Laser Look Out

Sometimes spies have to get past traps like this laser-beam tripwire. The laser beam is projected around the room by bouncing off mirrors then landing on a light sensor. If the beam is broken, an alarm is triggered. Beeeeep! It's a perfect way to protect your stuff! Places like banks and museums already use this technology. This room is divided up by lasers. Can you spy where each shape came from in the big picture? Careful, some are turned around.

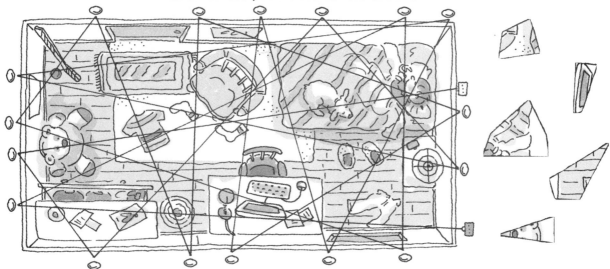

The EVERYTHING KIDS' SPIES Puzzle and Activity Book

Odd and Even

New cameras are being developed that not only record but also interpret what they see. Soon cameras may be able to tell from the way someone walks if they are hiding something or if they are a threat.

"Thermal imager" is the name spies use to describe a heat-sensitive surveillance video camera and display.

Can you tell what Mr. and Mrs. Odd are hiding? They have a total of 31 sets of numbers—14 of them are even, the rest are odd. Can you find which ones are which?

Scenes of the Crime!

Lots of techno-logical advances we use every day are thanks to spy work. Photo satellites, which deliver images in seconds around the world, were first used for intelligence gathering.

This is a surveillance photo of a crime scene. Somebody's changed things around! Can you see what's different? *

Did you hear about the thief who stole a calendar?

He got twelve months.

*Hint—12 things have been changed.

The EVERYTHING KIDS' SPIES Puzzle and Activity Book

Spies in Space

In the 1960s Russia and the United States studied having spies working in space. Rockets were even built for this purpose. Then both sides decided it was too expensive to put people in space when the work could be done by unmanned satellites. In the future, it is certain that spies will do their work among the stars. Can you see what these spies have discovered?

A spy took some pictures of Mars and Saturn. He got the best of both worlds!

How to Spot a Spy

Draw what you think a spy looks like.

What does a spy look like??
Of course there's no exact answer to what a spy looks like, but studies have shown they are often 21–35 years old. They are just as often men as women and have a very rich imagination.

Spy Talk

Here are some words overheard at a spy convention—but they're all mixed up. Can you make sense of them? Then read the shaded letters to find out what every spy needs.

nug

decos

edggta

ocpeil

secacs

tpusces

aarcem

rectse

siuidges

iisonms

Window Shopping

They really are watching you!
A company in Japan has invented mannequins with tiny cameras hidden in them. They spy on customers and move to attract customers' attention. They also gather information such as what bags the person is carrying, their age, and whether they are male or female.

The shoppers below are very logical. Can you see what they should buy next?

a.

b.

c.

a.

b.

c.

a.

b.

c.

What's in a Name?
Billy's mother had three children.
The first child was named May.
The second child was named June.
What was the third child's name?

Nano Spy

The Department of Defense has plans to develop a nano plane in the shape of a maple tree seed. It will be remote-controlled and weigh only 0.07 ounces! The tiny camera inside will be used to collect military intelligence. It will fly like a maple-tree seed, spinning around on its blade while the camera stays stationary.

Nano: Nano is the next size down from "micro." It comes from the Greek word for "dwarf." It can also mean one billionth.

Here are some photos the nano-cam took. Photo "b" was taken one week after photo "a" and it looks like they removed some things. Can you find the 12 changes?

The EVERYTHING KIDS' SPIES Puzzle and Activity Book

Fashion Finder

GPS* devices are so small they can fit in a shoe. Soon they will be inserted in clothes like shirts and pants. Perfect for a spy who wants to track you. And finally you can find that sock that got lost in the dryer!

Just like the word *track*, each thing on this page has the letters "ck" in it. Can you figure out all the words?

_ _ _ _ c k

_ _ c k _ _

_ _ c k

_ _ c k _ _

_ _ c k

_ _ c k _ _

_ _ c k _ _

_ _ c k

*GPS means Global Positioning System.
It is a way to track a person's position using satellites and a device on the person.

Resources about Spying: Web Sites, Books, Etc.

✎*www.intelligencesearch.com/* A helpful site focused on "underground espionage Web sites." Some very useful things, like words only spies use and how to understand them.

✎*www.forties.net/wwIIfemalespies.html* This site tells you all about some female heroes you have probably never heard about even though they have changed the way you live.

✎*www.klast.net/bond/* Everything you would ever want to know about James Bond—and more. This site tells all about the famous fictional character, who created him, and who played him in all the movies.

✎*www.spymuseum.org/* Did you know there is a real spy museum located in Washington, D.C.? This site gives a lot of information on the history of spying in America and all the different tricks of the trade.

✎*http://mprofaca.cro.net/spyanimals.html* Animals have been called in for years to help us spy, and this site tells you all about some of the crazy things we have made them do for us.

✎*www.nsa.gov/kids/home.cfm* This site is great if you like to play games or learn how to do codes. Lots of fun!

✎*http://enwikipedia.org/wiki/Category:Spies* Wikipedia is a great place to begin learning about spies. It has a whole section devoted to the world of spies.

✎*www.thunk.com/* Here's a fun site all about codes and secret messages—for kids only!

✎*www.gizmag.com/spygear/* Do you like gizmos and gadgets? This is the site for you, and real-life spies!

Appendix B
Puzzle Solutions

Bond, James Bond • page 2

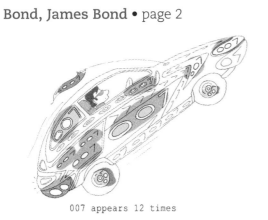

007 appears 12 times

He woke up oily the next morning

Get Smarter! • page 3

Groovyyy... • page 4

Lights, Camera, Spy! • page 4

In the Shadows • page 5

I Spy with My Little Eye • page 6

Just add a Y and they all make a word.
fly, dry, spy, cry why

Live + Let Lie • page 7

This character speaks so quietly they call him 'Whisper'

Rosie Carver was a rogue agent from the CIA

Tee Hee Johnson got his name because he laughed for no real reason

Baron Samedi was the henchman for the famous Mr. Big

Ruby Cutter   Shouter   Boo Hoo Wilson   Earl Lundi

The year reads the same upside down or right side up!

Mall Mission • page 8

Did you want the egg salad or chicken sandwich chief?

Spy on the Run • page 9

She got to the other slide

Top Secret Tools • page 9

video
knife
traps
codes

The **EVERYTHING KIDS** SPIES Puzzle and Activity Book

V.I.P. SPY • page 10

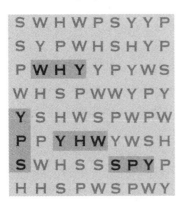

Saintly Spy • page 11

Spy at Sea • page 12

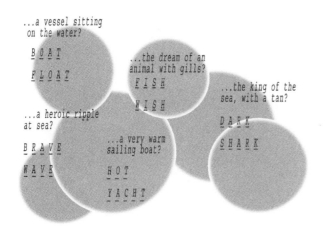

...a vessel sitting
on the water?

B O A T

F L O A T

...the dream of an
animal with gills?

F I S H

W I S H

...the king of the
sea, with a tan?

D A R K

S H A R K

...a heroic ripple
at sea?

B R A V E

W A V E

...a very warm
sailing boat?

H O T

Y A C H T

Dress Up Disguise • page 14

He had to, he was hiding behind the chicken.

Tick, Tick, Tick . . . • page 15

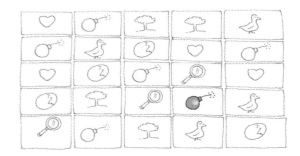

Egyptian Espionage • page 16

The secret message is:

By the Pyramid at noon

Appendix B: Puzzle Solutions

113

Spies in the House . . . • page 16

A giant potted plant

Night Vision • page 17

1. 5 PEOPLE ARE WEARING SUNGLASSES.
2. THE SIGN SAYS 'NO PICTURES'
3. THE GUARD'S GUN IS ON HIS LEFT SIDE.
4. THE OTHER PAINTING IS OF A TREE.
5. 2 PEOPLE ARE TALKING ON THEIR PHONES.
6. 3 PEOPLE HAVE BACKPACKS.
7. THE MOON IS NOT FULL.

See You Laterrrrr . . . • page 18

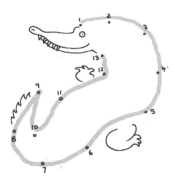

It means "Lizard" and that is how we came to call it the alligator.

Dumpster Diving • page 19

From the desk of Auntie Mildred

Attn:
E.V.I.L.
Headquarters
123 Dastardly Lane
Badville, Ickyland

Dear Big Honcho,

Delivery is on schedule for secret plans at Red Owl. Agent Poppycock will be there at 14:00 hours as arranged.
Payment must be in small unmarked bills - delivered in a blue and yellow suitcase with wheels.
Or else!!

Sincerely yours,
Auntie Mildred

Have a nice day!

Stop imagining!
:)

Gadget Magic! • page 20

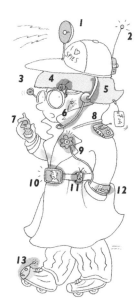

The nickname for the first atomic bomb was 'Gadget'.

The EVERYTHING KIDS' SPIES Puzzle and Activity Book

Sp-eye Glasses • page 21

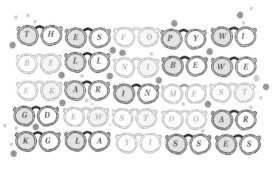

THE SPY WILL BE WEARING DARK GLASSES

They were married.

What Are You Looking At? • page 22

A spy ring

Spy Buster • page 23

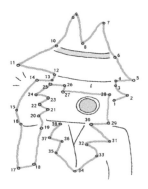

Spy Sweep • page 23

Dusting the room looking for fingerprints

Inspecting for bugging devices and cameras

Installing energy efficient lightbulbs

Having a short nap

Deadly Do-Right • page 24

Hear Kitty Kitty! • page 26

SPY
CAT

Appendix B: Puzzle Solutions

Licensed to Smell • page 27

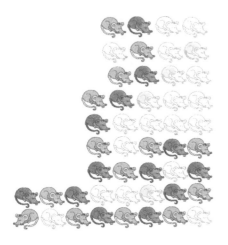

Sneaky Storks • page 28

Dinosaurs were around long before chickens existed so the answer is the egg.

Doggy Don't • page 29

Who's Watching Who? • page 30

don't look now but

there's a spy behind you

Secret Mission • page 30

 (a)  + et

p +

bullet proof
vest

(b)  +

sunglasses

(c)  +

crowbar

Pigeon Crime! • page 31

These were real jail birds! During World War 11, two pigeons were held as prisoners of war by the British after being captured from Nazi Germany.

White. It had to be a polar bear otherwise the spy would have been 3 miles from his camp.

The EVERYTHING KIDS' SPIES Puzzle and Activity Book

Cold War, Warm Bomb • page 32

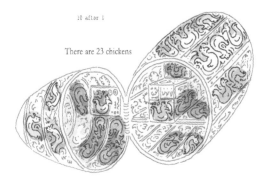

10 after 1

There are 23 chickens

You win if you carry on as normal. Chickens don't know what bombs are.

Pigeon Mission Grounded! • page 33

A carrier
pigeon can
fly 50 mph

Spy Sharks! • page 34

A jellybutton

Follow the Lion Line • page 35

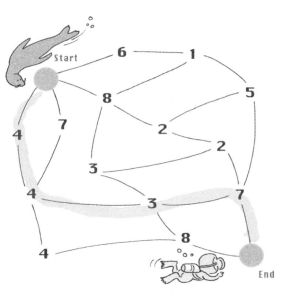

Bird Brains • page 36

BIRD BRAINS

A: MISSION ACCOMPLISHED

B: TIME SPENT IN THE AIR

C: BRAVERY

D: ABILITY TO DECODE MESSAGES

G.I. Joe 10601   Scotch-Lass   Ruhr-Express   Snow White

The other names were also heroic pigeons from World War Two.

Appendix B: Puzzle Solutions

Spy at Sea • page 37

Double Cross • page 41

Talk the Talk • page 37

Raven is a female agent
Chicken feed is low grade information
Hunting Pack is a surveillance team
Mole is an undercover agent

Name That Code • page 42

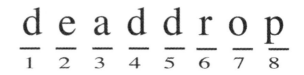

Dot, Dash, D'Oh! • page 40

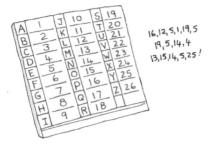

Please send money!

Detective to the Rescue! • page 42

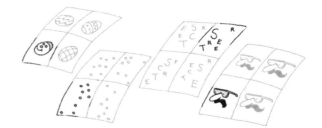

The EVERYTHING KIDS' SPIES Puzzle and Activity Book

Spy Camp • page 43

Don't Be Left Hanging! • page 44

If you're working for both sides you're a douBle agent.

One of Nathan Hale's first jobs was as a teacheR.

Another name for an operation is a mIssion.

A spy is also known as a secreT agent.

The U.S. security service is called the c.I.a.

If you dress up like somebody else it's called a diSguise.

You saved a life, you're a Hero!

Nathan Hale was a capTain in the army.

If the enemy captures you, you're a pRisoner.

A decOy distracts from the real thing.

The place they hang people is called the gallOws.

Somebody you don't trust is called a susPect.

To light a bomb you need a fuSe.

Nathan Hale was spying on the BRITISH TROOPS

Medieval Messenger • page 45

Switch the E for O, the M for W and the S for R

You will be met by Sir Randolph on his horse. You **must be ready to ride to the middle of town at midnight Saturday!** *

* This is written in code

Turn the page upside down. If you want to do this at home all you need is some paper and crayons. The trick to making an upside down face is to have a hat (it can look like a chin) and a beard (it can look like a hat.)

Caesar Cipher • page 46

BRING ME A SALAD!

Because he wanted to go Roman

Speedy Spartans • page 47

Beware spies are everywhere
Only trust this messenger!

N for November

Spy Queens • page 48

22 magnifying glasses
23 eyeglasses

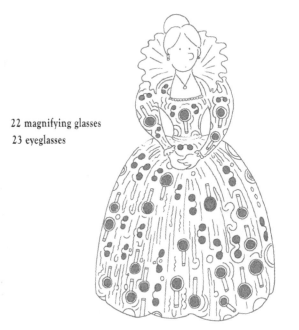

What, What? • page 50

Currency Affair • page 50

23-8-1-20 8-1-19 1 8-5-1-4, 1 20-1-9-12, 9-19
What has a head, a tail, is

2-18-15-23-14 2-21-20 8-1-19 14-15 12-5-7-19?
brown but has no legs?

a penny

The Scarf Knows • page 49

Muddled Mail • page 52

The EVERYTHING KIDS' SPIES Puzzle and Activity Book

Crossword Cross Border • page 53

Across

3. Somebody owns you

4. Not one but...

5. The night before

6. Walk don't ...

Down

1. The person in charge

2. A brave woman is a ...

3. She watches secretly.

Coded Crossword • page 54

Across
1 If you break it you can use it
7 Not stop but...
9 If you're from the USSR you are...
18 I can't tell you, it's a...

Down
1 What spies search for
5 Not lost but...
7 It's what you play

Shark No More • page 55

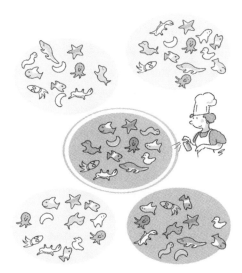

C.I.Eh? • page 54

France	DGSE
India	CBI
Russia	KGB
Canada	CSIS
Vietnam	CONG AN BO
USA	CIA

Silly Spy Sayings • page 56

six spies sneak
slowly south

leader looks
like lady

frightening
females fight foes

dirty double
drops decoy

agent aims
at america

Appendix B: Puzzle Solutions

The Great Escape • page 56

Untie the Spy • page 58

Spy Dance • page 57

The EVERYTHING KIDS' SPIES Puzzle and Activity Book

You've Been Warned! • page 59

ink	pine	spit	torn
one	rip	skin	tone
neon	riot	sip	tons
nip	rose	stone	tip
note	rink	sore	
pin	spot	sink	
pint	spin	store	

And the Award Goes To . . . • page 60

BOW TIE	**BIKINI**	**SHAWL**
DRESSING GOWN	**ROBE**	**KILT**
SPACE SUIT	**KIMONO**	**COAT**
BOARD SHORTS	**BLOUSE**	**APRON**
DAISY DUKES	**TOGA**	**HAT**
OVEN MITT	**HOODIE**	**SWEATPANTS**
SKI SUIT	**BEANIE**	**CAP**
RAIN COAT	**CAPE**	**LOINCLOTH**

THE SPY ONLY WEARS CLOTHES WITH TWO WORDS	**THE ACTOR ONLY WEARS' CLOTHES THAT END IN A VOWEL**	**THE CLOWN ONLY WEARS CLOTHES THAT END IN A CONSONANT**

Starstruck! • page 61

The plane leaves tonight
It's a long dark flight
Tomorrow it will be light
And Paris will be a great sight!

Spy-focals!

All Star! • page 64

Not a crocodile but an...
ALLIGATOR

It makes you sneeze
ALLERGY

A narrow street
ALLEY

To let do something
ALLOW

To attract
ALLURE

To frighten
STARTLE

To be very hungry
STARVE

Looking directly
STARING

A small bird
STARLING

It has five arms
STARFISH

Appendix B: Puzzle Solutions

123

$pyPay • page 65

$PY PAY

He had a chicken under surveillance.

Secret Sight • page 66

NIGHT VISION

You'll just have to be a little patient.

Great Gizmos! • page 66

Great Gizmos!

The **EVERYTHING KIDS** SPIES **Puzzle and Activity Book**

License to Spy • page 67

I SPY FOR YOU	SUPER SECRET	ESPIONAGE
GREAT WAITER	UNDERCOVER	DISGUISE EXPERT

This license plate belongs to a waiter not a spy.

Spy School • page 68

Apple
Bear
Cow
Dog
Eel
Frog
Goat
Horse
Icicle
Jar
Key
Lamb
Mouse
Nun
Owl
Pear
Queen
Robot
Snake
Teacup
Umbrella
Vampire
Waiter
Xylophone
Zebra

NameGame • page 69

Luke	Wendy
Elaine	Dave
Peter	Sam
Miranda	Frank
Yolanda	Ruth
Victor	Quentin
Brian	Nancy
Chris	Orville
Gerry	Uma
Julie	Ian
Tony	Harry
Xavier	Allan
Zac	Kelly

Secret List • page 70

LOCK
ROPE
BOOTS
DISGUISE
LASER

Appendix B: Puzzle Solutions

The Spy Twins • page 71

Mata Hari - A Dutch spy and dancer in World War 1
Nathan Hale - An American hero who spied on the British
James Bond - Agent 007 was created by writer Ian Fleming
Tokyo Rose - She never existed but Iva Toguri went to prison for her crimes

Risky Business • page 73

There are 37 ice cream cones.

A tennis ball.

Six Spies • page 72

There are 5 of these

There are 7 of this

Ancient Agents • page 76

The EVERYTHING KIDS' SPIES Puzzle and Activity Book

Bird's-Eye View • page 77

Country Code • page 79

FRANCE ITALY CHINA JAPAN SPAIN
IRAN GREECE PAKISTAN INDIA BRAZIL
ENGLAND CANADA

I C E L A N D

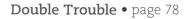

Double Trouble • page 78

BECAUSE HE WAS A DIRTY DOUBLE CROSSER

By Norse code!

Appendix B: Puzzle Solutions

In Plain View • page 79

Treason, betrayal, criminal, prisoner, decoy.

A Head of His Time • page 80

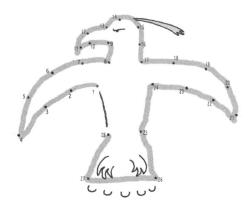

Micro What? • page 82

PETITE
MINUTE
LITTLE

Because the bed wouldn't come to him!

Don't Look Now • page 81

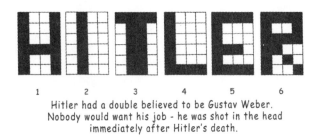

Hitler had a double believed to be Gustav Weber.
Nobody would want his job - he was shot in the head
immediately after Hitler's death.

It's a Bird, It's a Bee, It's a Plane!!! • page 83

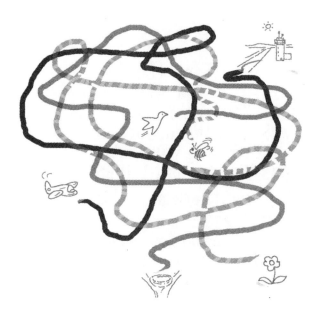

Skeleton Secrets • page 84

watch
handkerchief
shaving tube
studs
toothbrush
fountain pen
compass
flashlight
box of matches

Bone appetite!

Appendix B: Puzzle Solutions

Inside Job • page 85

Close Call • page 85

Gadget Girl • page 88

Mirror Code • page 89

MeeT mE OnlinE tOniGht
at 18:00 aNd I wiLl
shoW You the WeBsitE
i waS taLKINg abOUt.
BesuRe tO briNg **your NeW
paSsWoRd. uNtiL thEN**
yOu   muSt rememBEr this
SECRET PHRASE:

*the caMel will swim
tO the River on Sunday
evE.*

MORSE   Street signs are
examples of codes.

The EVERYTHING KIDS' SPIES Puzzle and Activity Book

When Bats Attack! • page 90

HEROISM

DARING

SPIRIT

BOLDNESS

GALLANTRY

CHAMPION

FEARLESS

A high dry spy.

Killer Spy Robots • page 92

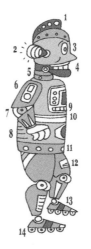

In a mini van!

Trace That Call • page 91

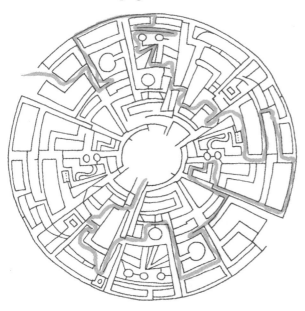

Cat Vision • page 93

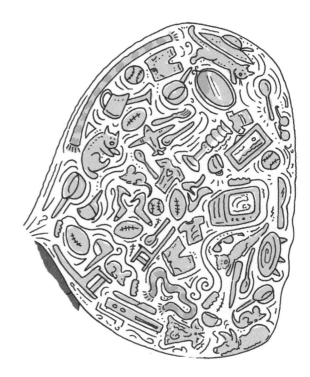

Appendix B: Puzzle Solutions

Robot Spies • page 94

CATFISH

Hack Attack! • page 95

CALL ME
WHEN YOU
GET HOME
AND WE CAN
GO TO THE
MALL.

Footfall • page 95

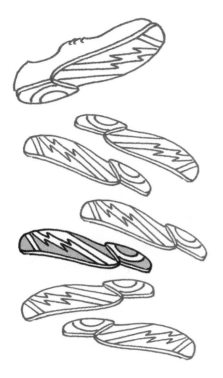

Raise the Flag • page 94

347**F**559**A**77**L**
394**S**98569**E**3
6**F**9923564**L**4
447689**A**2288
234**G**7768992

Great Gadgets! • page 96

dEcoy
ciA
eNigma
fliP
doubLe
rcmP
ninjaS
sneakY

S P Y P L A N E

Seeing Double • page 89

Nine

The EVERYTHING KIDS' SPIES Puzzle and Activity Book

Seagull or Spyplane? • page 100

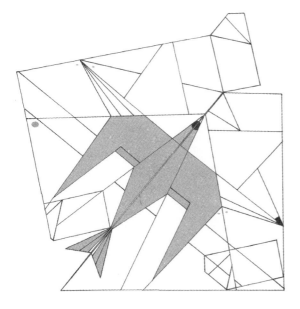

Future Spy • page 102

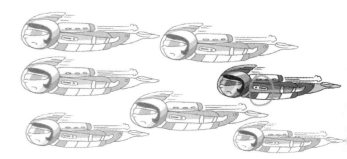

Secret Cipher • page 101

Laser Look Out • page 102

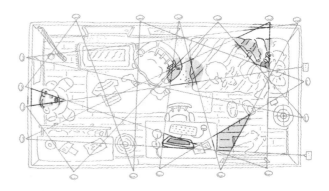

Appendix B: Puzzle Solutions

Odd and Even • page 103

There's 17 odd totals and 14 even totals

Spies in Space • page 105

Scenes of the Crime! • page 104

The **EVERYTHING KIDS'** SPIES Puzzle and Activity Book

Spy Talk • page 106

gun

codes

gadget

police

access

suspect

camera

disguise

secret

mission

What every spy
needs is:
'Sunglasses'

Window Shopping • page 107

b.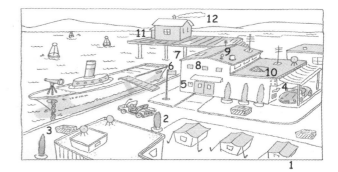

c.

c.

That would be Billy.
He's the third child.

Nano Spy • page 108

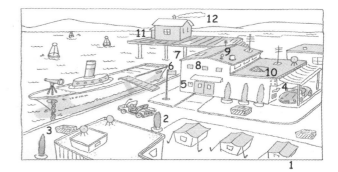

Fashion Finder • page 109

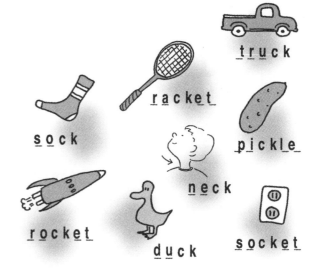

_t r u c k

r a c k e t_

_s o_ c k

_p i c k l e_

n _e_ c k

_r o c k e t_

_d u_ c k

_s o c k e t_

The Everything® KIDS' Series!

Packed with tons of information, activities, and puzzles, the Everything® Kids' books are perennial bestsellers that keep kids active and engaged.

Each book is two-color, 8" x 9¼", and 144 pages.

The Everything® Kids' Fairies Book
1-59869-394-8, $7.95

The Everything® Kids' Magical Science Experiments Book
1-59869-426-X, $7.95

The Everything® Kids' Environment Book
1-59869-670-X, $7.95

The Everything® Kids' Racecars Puzzle and Activity Book
1-59869-243-7, $7.95

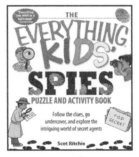

The Everything® Kids' Spies Puzzle and Activity Book
1-59869-409-X, $7.95

A silly, goofy, and undeniably icky addition to
the Everything® Kids' series . . .

The Everything® Kids'
GROSS
Series

Chock–full of sickening entertainment for hours of disgusting fun.

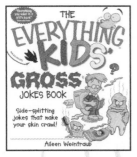

The Everything® Kids'
Gross Jokes Book
1-59337-448-8, $7.95

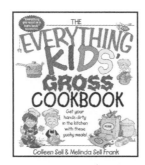

The Everything® Kids'
Gross Cookbook
1-59869-324-7, $7.95

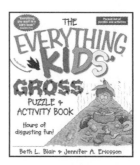

The Everything® Kids' Gross
Puzzle & Activity Book
1-59337-447-X, $7.95

The Everything® Kids'
Gross Mazes Book
1-59337-616-2, $7.95

The Everything® Kids' Gross
Hidden Pictures Book
1-59337-615-4, $7.95

Other Everything® Kids' Titles Available

The Everything® Kids' Animal Puzzle & Activity Book
1-59337-305-8

The Everything® Kids' Baseball Book, 4th Ed.
1-59337-614-6

The Everything® Kids' Bible Trivia Book
1-59337-031-8

The Everything® Kids' Bugs Book
1-58062-892-3

The Everything® Kids' Cars and Trucks
Puzzle & Activity Book
1-59337-703-7

The Everything® Kids' Christmas Puzzle
& Activity Book
1-58062-965-2

The Everything® Kids' Cookbook
1-58062-658-0

The Everything® Kids' Crazy Puzzles Book
1-59337-361-9

The Everything® Kids' Dinosaurs Book
1-59337-360-0

The Everything® Kids' First Spanish Puzzle & Activity Book
1-59337-717-7

The Everything® Kids' Halloween Puzzle &
Activity Book
1-58062-959-8

The Everything® Kids' Hidden Pictures Book
1-59337-128-4

The Everything® Kids' Horses Book
1-59337-608-1

The Everything® Kids' Joke Book
1-58062-686-6

The Everything® Kids' Knock Knock Book
1-59337-127-6

The Everything® Kids' Learning Spanish Book
1-59337-716-9

The Everything® Kids' Math Puzzles Book
1-58062-773-0

The Everything® Kids' Mazes Book
1-58062-558-4

The Everything® Kids' Money Book
1-58062-685-8

The Everything® Kids' Nature Book
1-58062-684-X

The Everything® Kids' Pirates Puzzle and Activity Book
1-59337-607-3

The Everything® Kids' Presidents Book
1-59869-262-3

The Everything® Kids' Princess Puzzle & Activity Book
1-59337-704-5

The Everything® Kids' Puzzle Book
1-58062-687-4

The Everything® Kids' Riddles & Brain Teasers Book
1-59337-036-9

The Everything® Kids' Science Experiments Book
1-58062-557-6

The Everything® Kids' Sharks Book
1-59337-304-X

The Everything® Kids' Soccer Book
1-58062-642-4

The Everything® Kids' States Book
1-59869-263-1

The Everything® Kids' Travel Activity Book
1-58062-641-6

All titles are $6.95 or $7.95 unless otherwise noted.

Available wherever books are sold!
To order, call 800-258-0929, or visit us at *www.adamsmedia.com*
Everything® and everything.com® are registered trademarks of F+W Publications, Inc.
Prices subject to change without notice.